Learning Moments for Evolving Leaders

Providing leaders and their colleagues with inspiration - or reminders - regarding the critical role leaders play in the lives of employees.

Michael Holland

2013

Bishop House Consulting
INCORPORATED

Now all glory to God, who is able, through his mighty power at work within us, to accomplish infinitely more than we might ask or think.

Ephesians 3:20 (NLT)

Table of Contents

Introduction

Great leaders leverage opportunities to create deep self-awareness of their personal leadership style and build cohesive teams through trusted relationships. The *Leadership Learning Moments* contained in this book will prompt leaders at all levels of maturity to think about their leadership style, their relationships, and the impact they could have within their organization.

As you read through these pages, take the time to reflect on your core management behavior, and consider the tweaks you could make in your leadership habits that would make you more effective.

Lead Well!

Michael Holland
Founder/President, Bishop House Consulting, Inc.

Learning Moments

The Role of a Leader

Learning Moments

Create Organizational Clarity

I imagine that most employees can recite the general wording of the mission statement or vision statement or whatever statement is posted around their work environment. In our own lives we all have statements we've memorized: the Pledge of Allegiance, scouting pledges, the Lord's Prayer, the first few phrases of Lincoln's Gettysburg Address, the 1975 McDonalds jingle "two all-beef patties special sauce . . ." But there's a distinct difference between someone reciting a statement and someone living the essence and purpose behind that statement. Somehow, there is a deeper connection to the intent of the statement.

The psyche of successful teams and companies centers on the concept of all members knowing intimately the purpose and intent of the entity. The employees or team members know their individual roles and how those roles help to achieve success for the greater good. This intimate knowledge comes from leaders who work hard to create, sustain and protect organizational clarity, which according to author Patrick Lencioni ". . . [is] not merely about choosing the right words to describe a company's mission, strategy or values; it is about agreeing on the fundamental concepts that drive it."

Your role as a leader is to work with your peers to create organizational clarity, allowing employees to really know why the team and organization exists, whom it serves and what is to be achieved, then to behave and lead in ways that amplify those fundamental concepts.

What Will I Do When. . .

As a leader, you may ultimately be faced with a situation that you never would have believed could happen. A leader is charged with so much responsibility and often has little training or wisdom to deal with the challenges that life can bring. The list below contains real situations I, or leaders I know, have faced.

- An employee with a terminal diagnosis.

- An employee showing visible signs of physical abuse.

- An employee informing you that his local family has just found out that he fathered 2 kids in a foreign country, whose mother now wants to bring those kids to the US.

- A peer manager committing suicide.

- An employee alerting you to the fact that her deranged and abusive husband is coming to the office with a weapon in a jealous rage over a perceived interoffice relationship.

- A boss announcing a pending marriage to their same sex partner.

- An employee losing a child to illness, a car accident, or suicide.

- An employee borrowing against his retirement account to send his teenager to an extremely expensive, specialized rehab center in an effort to save his child's life.

- An employee losing her home to foreclosure.

Sometimes as leaders we know our employees on a deep level and what's happening in their life and the lives of those around them, but more often we only know what's going on at the surface. And while policies, regulations, laws, protocol, leadership books, and management training are all well and good in educating and guiding us on what's supposed to occur in a given situation, at some point as a leader you will be faced with a situation that will challenge every fiber of your emotional well-being.

You can't be fully prepared for all situations, but you can seed some behaviors that may help you provide comfort and support to an employee or a peer or a boss. Use the situations in the list above to act out the ensuing conversations and visualize your actions/behaviors/ mannerisms, allowing you to "see it before you do it." Gain insight regarding how your emotions may overwhelm you and which situations may be more difficult due to you own life experiences.

The Gap in Leadership Capacity

Assessing the impact of an organization's leadership reveals an odd, almost indescribable foggy, murky blob of an answer. We can plot out a nifty graph that shows the maturity of leaders based on facts about time in the role, education, depth and breadth of assignments, success of attaining metrics, employee retention, performance, etc. More difficult though is the calculation of leadership wisdom defined as what leaders gained from their experiences, which they in turn translate into better leadership in the future. Further, if we could accumulate the valuable buckets of leadership wisdom across the organization, would we then have a true measure of the real maturity of the leadership asset with the organization?

We believe, and studies have shown, there is this appreciating – or depreciating – asset of leadership. We also believe and know that wise leaders at any level in an organization have an amplified positive impact on employee engagement. Therefore, if we increase this wisdom, we likely increase the value of our asset and, conversely, if the wisdom decreases then the value of the asset likely decreases.

So, maybe the real concern should center on understanding the opportunity cost we incur with regard to the size of the leadership capacity gap. That gap would be the difference in value of the leadership asset today and the value at full capacity.

To Think About

What if we could leverage 8% or 10% more of the nebulous leadership capacity, resulting in leaders being wiser, thereby engaging employees more deeply who then passionately impact customers? How might your bottom line be impacted?

G.R.O.W.

Ken Blanchard has a new book out. You might remember Blanchard, who wrote the now classic, *The One Minute Manager*, which was extremely impactful, given it's easy to read format and 3 practical management techniques.

The new book, *Great Leaders GROW*, is an easy read business fable. I like the simplicity with which he approaches the complex world of leadership by challenging that leadership isn't something you learn in a day. Great leaders become great because they are on a long journey to learn and increase their wisdom. Here's a summary of his model.

G = Gain Knowledge

R = Reach Out to Others

O = Open Your World

W = Walk Towards Wisdom

I've come to the conclusion that a journey for leadership wisdom is like being a successful parent: you can fake caring but you can't fake showing up. Being labeled as the parent of a kid is substantially different than actively engaging in creating a sustainable relationship, exacting measured counseling versus discipline, and committing to showing up every day.

If you are going through the motions as a leader, then you aren't creating leadership wisdom, nor are you being as effective as you could be. And if this is the case and you are really a stand-up guy or gal, you would ask the company to reduce your compensation package to more appropriately match your value to the organization.

Leadership Archaeologist

The interesting thing about people coming together in organizations is that they tend to create a mini-society and this society will have its own personality, rules, values and behaviors. Leaders may tend to underestimate the ingrained culture within these mini-societies and overestimate their ability to change these mini-societies with simple commands, just-in-time leadership and because they said so (always a great leadership approach.)

Consider adjusting your leadership perspective, taking on a temporary role of archaeologist. The discipline of archaeology involves surveyance, excavation and eventually analysis of data collected to learn more about past human activity. In broad scope, archaeology relies on cross-disciplinary research, drawing upon anthropology, history, art history, classics, ethnology, geography, geology, linguistics, semiology, physics, information sciences, chemistry, statistics, paleoecology, paleontology, paleozoology, paleoethnobotany, and paleobotany.

Learning more about your employees and their culture may just help you learn more about your leadership capability.

Leaders Leading Leaders

I recently finished John Maxwell's, *The 5 Levels of Leadership*. I'm struck by the simplicity and power he reveals in his model for describing the role leaders attempt to play. The simplicity of the 5 Levels – Position, Permission, Production, People Development, and Pinnacle – is a basic path through increase of power and influence. However, Maxwell's depth comes from painting a shift in paradigm with regard to how power and influence are wielded. Most intriguing for me is the movement from the 3rd Level, Production, a level revealing leaders making things happen and separating themselves from the pack with high production through a team or teams, to Level 4, a level summarized as developing leaders into leaders who can lead others.

Take a moment and re-read the last 8 words: developing leaders into leaders who can lead others. Think about the skill, maturity, and emotional intelligence gap which exists from leading teams to **produce** to developing leaders to **lead**. Becoming a great leader will require you to identify, grow, equip, and support leaders.

Ultimately, you lead well not through your perceived power, but through empowering others – other leaders as well as employees – who become successful because of the leadership you model.

Here's a rundown of Maxwell's 5 Levels:

> **Level 1: Position** – It's a great place to visit, but you won't want to stay there.

> **Level 2: Permission** – You can't lead people until you like people

> **Level 3: Production** – Making things happen separates real leaders from wannabes

Level 4: People Development – Helping individual leaders grow extends your influence and impact

Level 5: Pinnacle – The highest leadership accomplishment is developing other leaders to Level 4

Shine Through Leadership

Obstacles confront us daily. Leaders get the opportunity to not only overcome their own challenges, but to also guide others to persevere through/over/past their challenges.

Matt and Kim Shell are my new heroes. They are leaders of a very small team that in 2009 faced challenges that tested the deep reservoirs of all the wisdom gained through life. Through their leadership, they guided Jacob, one of their team members, to be a strong performer and successful in all that he was working towards.

While many of us are challenged during a typical week with managing overlapping meetings, solving people dynamics and juggling endless work deadlines, Jacob spent part of a week in 2009 delivering 59 million stem cells in his fight against neuroblastoma, a rare form of childhood cancer. Jacob, my redheaded neighbor and all of 8 years old at the time, reflected the strength, fortitude and positive energy that his parents, Matt and Kim, had instilled in him.

Impactful leaders walk the walk every day, revealing the behaviors and attitudes they expect of those who follow. Matt and Kim's leadership seemed all the norm before Jacob's illness. What shone through in 2009 was just how effective they had been as leaders of their small team/family over the 8 short years before Jacob's illness. Jacob's brilliance shone through with the simplicity of how to work through challenges one day at a time.

It's November 23, 2012 and today Matt Shell, head coach of the Burnt Hills High School football team, will lead our team onto the field for the NY State Championship Game. Thousands of fans will be watching the game at Syracuse University's Carrier Dome or on cable television. The game will be exciting; the tension high. Matt will be busy on the sideline leading, inspiring, and motivating the team. Every now and then we'll see the glimpse of an 11 year old redheaded kid roaming the sideline. And in the hearts of hundreds of young adults who have been students of Kim or Matt, or played on Matt's teams, and in the hearts of the rest of us, the brightness of great leadership will be revealed, forever solidified as a standard to which other leaders should be compared.

Your leadership impacts people every day and for years to come. Stand up and lead in ways that will shine through others.

For more of the Shell's story visit their website:
www.ShellstrongFoundation.org

Have You Jumped the Shark?

From the Urban Dictionary, the phrase "jumped the shark" is defined as: "the moment when something that was once great has reached a point where it will now decline in quality and popularity." The idiom's source is from an episode of the television show, Happy Days that went way too far in trying to keep its audience.

So, how do you know if you, as a leader, have jumped the shark? How would you know you are approaching the point at which you will jump the shark?

Signs that you may have jumped the shark as a leader. . .

- You are handing out the 58th Employee of the Month Award
- You don't notice that your employees are simply copying their annual goals from previous appraisals
- Employees consistently arrive late to your weekly staff meeting or simply don't bother to come
- You are way too comfortable handling employee terminations
- You are overly supportive of the across-the-board raises
- The last business book you read was *Good to Great* . . . in 2001 when it was released.
- Your motivational corporate speak is becoming punch lines at off-site employee gatherings
- Your employees have set up and consistently update a # on Twitter in your name
- You don't know what a # is or means, or how to find out

Take a moment and think this through. Are you engaged and leading your employees? Are they following you?

The Three Most Requested Leadership Practices

In a validation study for the *Everything DiSC® 363 for Leaders*, a tool we utilize to help leaders understand their impact on the organization, three leadership practices were consistently requested most often of leaders. The three most requested practices in order are:

1. **Stretching the Boundaries** – Pioneering leaders encourage the group to think creatively about its options and take chances on new opportunities, pushing beyond comfort zones and envisioning a new way of doing things.

2. **Rallying People to Achieve Goals** – Energizing leaders motivate people to see, feel, sense, grasp, and believe in a transcendent purpose.

3. **Improving Methods** – Resolute leaders seek success for their teams and the company in creating urgency around greater efficiency and seeking practical, common-sense approaches to innovate and constantly improve as a cultural norm.

Why are these three the most requested out of the possible 24 practices? Not sure. But possibly the more important question is why would most leaders not rate these as the practices as those *they believe* their employees, peers and bosses desire of them?

Our natural approach to leading emanates from our preferred communications style. We gain leadership wisdom as we lead daily, develop skills through training, and situationally review/assess the impacts of our decisions through the filter of our mentors and bosses. The leadership practices that come naturally are those which line up with your natural communications style. The other leadership practices need to be absorbed, learned and remembered. And this is why leadership is a job and not an entitlement.

DiSC® is a registered trademark of Inscape Publishing, Inc.

Get Naked to Build a Cohesive Team

How's the social cohesion within your team? To what extent are you and your team members really enjoying each other and relishing in each other's successes? Enjoying each other, now there's a concept! How on earth could I even begin to enjoy those people who seem to work so hard at making my life miserable?

A tremendous amount of time and energy is invested to create *appearances* of cohesion within teams – particularly management teams – while those teams struggle to reap the synergy of their wisdom. The art of building cohesive teams is really quite simple: build trusting relationships.

According to Patrick Lencioni, a renowned guru on the topic of teams, one of the most effective ways to build trust is a process he calls "getting naked." The critical component or outcome is for "team members to get comfortable with letting colleagues see them for who they are. No pretension. No positioning."

Be a leader and take the first step. Drop the act and be vulnerable with one of your peers. Let them get to know you better and seek to get to know them better.

Donate your talents. Reap rewards.

Back-to-back meetings all day. Family life waiting at home. Fifty new emails that should be read today. An employee really needs to talk with you ASAP. Leaders work hard every day. Can you find time to donate your talents to a good cause? Wait a minute, how on earth could you find any time to volunteer for another organization or group?

Volunteering just may provide a fantastic opportunity for you, as a leader, to gain a different perspective of your work.

- Working for an hour serving food to the homeless could provide the perspective that maybe that work situation isn't as bad as you thought.

- Coaching your daughter's soccer team might just give you the chance to try out some communication tools that could be used in your office.

- Spending time with your church leaders on the annual budget might help you think through how to do more with less and still meet your objectives.

- Investing your time to serve on a not-for-profit BOD might help you to develop the collaboration skills which seem to always be identified as a performance opportunity on your annual review.

- Sharing time talking with critically ill children might help you soften your verbal and non-verbal communication style with employees.

In the end, maybe you should be asking, how can I NOT lend my time, talent and energy to needy groups, people or organizations? The time invested could help to build your leadership wisdom and just might provide you with a little inspiration.

Take a Fresh Look

Your employee has asked to see you for a couple of minutes. Your instincts jump and your soul is telling you that it is likely the employee is going to resign. The meeting is as you thought; the employee has accepted a new position.

This is a great opportunity... for you and your team! This forced change provides the chance to look at the position and the role with fresh eyes. Don't merely replace the employee in-kind, *assuming* that the responsibilities and skills are still what you need. Look at the responsibilities and interactions the role had within your team, with internal customers, and with external customers. Is this an opportunity to create short-term, special projects for remaining employees who can gain new experiences? Take the time to truly assess the position and needs and opportunities.

Answer these questions. . .

- Are there changes in responsibilities or tasks that I would like to make?

- Is there other work I would like to incorporate into the position?

- Are there tasks that are no longer necessary?

- How does the position support the future goals for my team?

- Are there short-term projects that other members of my team could handle?

Adjust your mindset from "hiring a replacement" to "acquiring a talent asset" to signify the criticality of the process.

Who's on 1st, What's on 2nd

Build consistency in your leadership and delegation of tasks and projects by clearly differentiating the roles people should play. It's important to clarify that roles are not people.

Leaders must distinguish, clearly articulate and consistently visualize the differences between the roles that exist and the people who fulfill those roles.

One great tool to help identify and communicate roles and responsibilities is a project management approach code named RACI. RACI is a responsibility matrix and stands for Responsible, Accountable, Consulted and Informed. Below are descriptions for each role, copied directly from Wikipedia.

Responsible – Those who do the work to achieve the task. There is typically one role with a participation type of Responsible, although others can be delegated to assist in the work required.

Accountable (also Approver or final Approving Authority) – The one ultimately answerable for the correct and thorough completion of the deliverable or task, and the one from who Responsible is delegated the work. In other words, an Accountable must sign off (Approve) on work that Responsible provides. There must be only one Accountable specified for each task or deliverable.

Consulted (sometimes Counsel) – Those whose opinions are sought, typically subject matter experts; and with whom there is two-way communication.

Informed – Those who are kept up-to-date on progress, often only on completion of the task or deliverable; and with whom there is just one-way communication.

Give it a Try

Grab a blank piece of paper (or open Excel or Word) and create a table. Across the top, write the names of the people who are part of the project. Down the left side of the table, write the tasks or activities. Next, assign the roles using the RACI indicators for each task/activity by person. Think hard on the delineation of the roles and even more deeply on how well you've communicated those delineations among the folks who fulfill the roles.

The Traditions You Enable

What traditions have you created or enabled within your team or company? As a leader, you are in the powerful role of creating rituals, beliefs, values, and cultural norms by the ways in which you behave and enable behavior within others, both as individuals and in groups.

Tradition sounds so impressive and positive: the transmission of customs or beliefs that have been passed along over time. Sports teams have traditions, small towns have traditions, families have traditions, community groups have traditions, and faith-based groups have traditions.

But traditions can be negative as well. Ethnic/racial bias, union-management misperceptions, political party platforms, and economic vitality (think wealthy, middle class, lower middle class, poverty) have all negatively affected companies in the past and present.

So, what traditions will your legacy hold? What behaviors, customs, and beliefs are you enabling, with or without pre-thought? As you read the items below, think through how your employees talk about your legacy with their friends and family.

- Employee empowerment
- Growth from within
- Fear of layoffs
- Executive perks
- Trustworthiness
- Owner entitlement

- Professional growth
- Building future leaders
- Community volunteerism
- Profit, profit, profit
- Success
- Mediocrity

Where Does The Boss Spend His Time?

In a moment, the perception of how President Barrack Obama spends his time was vastly changed. The raid and killing of the infamous terrorist Bin Laden revealed the depth and breadth of critical and non-critical activities the President was involved in over the last several months. The juggling of information, decisions and moving projects/agendas forward is evident in the contrast of his leadership activities.

As we lead our companies and teams, we are constantly placed in positions where we must manage secretive and/or not-ready-for-prime-time information. The appearance of what we have going on is never the full picture.

- We know ahead of time that we will fire that manager down the hall.

- We may know for weeks or months that a transaction is forthcoming and when it closes, we will be telling many people they are "the synergies" sought to fund the deal (their jobs will be eliminated).

- We may know ahead of time the company will be giving raises this year though they will be very small and unpopular.

- We may know that one of our staff is dealing with a physical domestic abuse situation and that's why we are allowing her so much flexibility in her schedule.

- We may know about the future promotion of the top-notch manager before it is announced.

You may question the depth and breadth of work your boss or peers appear to be investing in the company. But I believe you should first ask yourself this: how much freedom from judgment am I allowing for my boss and peers and employees when I don't know – nor should I know – everything that is going on.

It may be best to work off this premise: accept and believe in your superior as you'd like your team and employees to accept and believe in you.

How Emotionally Strong is Your Team?

I recently delivered a speech on emotional intelligence – the ability to recognize and understand emotions in yourself and others, and your ability to use this awareness to manage your behavior and relationships – to an audience of senior executives and provided them with insight regarding how they can assess and grow their emotional intelligence (EI). For leaders, a key aspect of EI is the opportunity and challenge to harmonize emotions and thought, and then manage behavior. The investment of energy to understand/assess your EI can be doable at 9:30 in the morning but is much more difficult at 2:30 pm after 4 back-to-back meetings and no lunch.

A really interesting aspect of EI is to then ponder your team's EI. Further, how does the team's cumulative EI impact team performance?

Try this non-scientific approach: At your next team huddle, ask each person to describe the one or two things that scare them today. As team members respond, look for their level of vulnerability, for their trust in the group, and for their confidence in managing their emotion regarding the issue/item and maybe most importantly their capability to articulate their message.

Are You Having an Impact?

Effective leaders seek to continuously improve how they impact the organization and those with whom they interact. Gaining objective insight on your behaviors and how those behaviors impact others can provide you with critical data to adjust your actions and behaviors. So, where do you really stand? Are you an impactful leader? Is that a positive impact or a negative impact? When was the last meaningful conversation you had with your boss regarding how you are performing as a leader?

Seek the feedback. A profound method for analyzing how well you are doing is to seek feedback from individuals within various stakeholder groups that surround you. As a leader, you have your direct reports who have a perception of you. And there's the boss who has her own perception as well. But there are several other groups who can provide valuable insight.

- Peers – locally and globally
- Customers – external as well as internal
- Matrix team members – up, across and down
- Members of the Board of Directors, Mentors, External Advisors

Formal feedback can be garnered via a 360 degree feedback survey – think of yourself as at the center of the circle and your stakeholders surround you laterally, above and below – which provides tremendous, objective and usually anonymous feedback. Well-run 360 degree surveys provide the input along leadership competencies which allow you to internalize the perceptions from various stakeholders. Short on your budget? Here are some less formal methods you could follow to gain input.

- Create your own electronic survey and deploy to your stakeholders via

- o Free survey tool: www.Surveymonkey.com
- o Outlook Exchange Voting/Tracking Survey
- Create a simple questionnaire and email to your stakeholders
- Facilitate in-person meetings with stakeholders

To be successful, you should:

- Seek the feedback
- Create an action plan
- Find an accountability partner; your boss is a good place to start

Take Action

Take 4 minutes to determine your stakeholders. Using a blank piece of paper, draw a circle in the middle of the page the size of a half-dollar. Place your name in the circle. Now, draw spokes off of that circle and write the names of stakeholders. Start with broad groupings if needed such as direct reports, bosses, peers. Then narrow those groupings with individual names or subsets.

By taking inventory of your stakeholders, you will at least begin to think through how they might perceive your leadership impact on the organization.

Learning Moments

Evolving Your Skills

Learning Moments

Own Your Week

There's a point in time when you have to decide if you will take ownership of your time or allow the beast (the company, the boss, the customer, the colleague, the employees, the family) to own you and your time. Awhile back, I adjusted my perspective from seeing time as a critical asset, depleting every second, to a perspective of time being a tremendous investment opportunity, awaiting my direction.

A great blog post last year helped me to take a new look at how to "theme out" the week, akin to time blocking but with more substance. The concept is to create broad themes for large blocks of time in the day *and* themes for each day of the week. Here are the writer's broad themes:

- Broad Themes for the Waking Hours

    o Self - 5:00 am to 8:00 am

    o Work - 8:30 am to 6:00 pm

    o Family & Other - 6:30 pm to 9:00 pm

- Broad Themes by the Day

    o Monday - Team meetings; direct reports and team huddle

    o Tuesday & Wednesday - Extended meetings and travel themed out further by weeks of the month. So Week 1 is travel for these days while Week 4 is for ad hoc meetings.

    o Thursday - Ad hoc and lunch meetings

    o Friday - Planning and lunch meetings

    o Saturday - Personal

    o Sunday - Church

31

The exercise of reorganizing your time and schedule reaps the rewards more than the final picture or plan. Tweaking your habits and approach to the investment of time motivates your brain muscles to re-sync with your priorities, which have also been adjusted slightly or dramatically, depending on how satisfied you have been with your blended time allocation.

Creating Presence With Your GDT

Leading GDTs – Geographically Dispersed Teams – is more the norm for leaders today than an anomaly. Leaders leading teams spread across the USA or the world is surprisingly much the same as leading teams dispersed in several local stores or on separate floors of a building. The broadness of the spread of the GDT is less important than the effort a leader invests in maintaining open and effective communication paths. The frequency and quality of these conversations is directly related to the maturity of the leader and not proximity. Good leadership is enabled by quality communications. Employees don't necessarily care how you communicate with them, but they intimately care about the quality of your communications and if you really care about them.

I find that leaders with close GDT (same floor or building) actually spend less time in quality communications because they believe they are always present. Leaders with broader GDTs realize they need to invest time in creating communication opportunities and absolutely these leaders have to be more diligent and creative in developing relationships.

The principles of management and leadership remain constant. Great, and even good leaders will find ways to create opportunity to apply the principles enabling their employees to be successful.

To Think About

Two 8-year-old boys are playing against each other in a soccer game on a beautiful Saturday afternoon. Throughout the game, one boy looks over to see his father constantly on his iPhone, responding to emails or talking on the phone. The opposing player looks over at his dad filming the game, which the boy knows is being fed via Skype to his mom, who is watching the game live while out of town.

Proximity helps. Ultimately, determination, leveraging tools & technology, and creating presence enable opportunity for great leadership.

Get Educated in 180 Seconds

Do you have 3 minutes? A tremendous array of leadership education materials can be accessed on the Wall Street Journal website for simply the price of the online edition and the investment of a few minutes.

The WSJ's *Lessons in Leadership* series contains step-by-step how-to's, WSJ stories and video interviews with CEOs on management and leadership topics. The CEO videos range from 40 seconds to several minutes and reveal great advice from current and former CEOs from companies such as American Express, Ford, Aetna, PWC, and UBS. The how-to guides provide nice primers on topics and quick tips for those with even the most over-booked schedules.

The site is divided into broad categories which are listed below.

Developing a Leadership Style	Strategy
Building a Workplace Culture	Execution
Recruiting, Hiring and Firing	Innovation
Managing Your People	Managing Change

Take Action

Spend the next 5 minutes signing up for the WSJ online and then watch one video in less than 2 minutes. Tomorrow, invest a few minutes reviewing the topics. Decide which might be valuable to you and which might be good to recommend to someone on your team. Watch another short video.

The next day, read a how-to guide. During your commute home, take a few moments to think about the brief education snapshots from this week. Were they helpful? How did you apply the knowledge? What topic(s) creates curiosity for you?

13 Minutes a Day to Better Productivity

Are you investing 13 minutes a day planning your work? How about your employees?

Productivity increases significantly when we make conscious decisions about what to work on and for how long. Planning allows us to be proactive rather than reactive and to work for results rather than filling time fighting fires or just being busy with activities. Invest 13 minutes in planning and re-planning your day to stay focused and increase your and your team's productivity.

7 Minutes to Start Your Day

Start your day investing 7 minutes of your budget to think about the following:

- What **should** I be working on today to get the results I and my team need?
- Where am I **investing** my valuable time?
- What work will best **model behaviors** I expect in others?

Two, 2 Minute Time Outs

As the day progresses, continually ask the question "what is the best use of my time right now?" Establish two time-outs which you'll use to review your plan and adjust your focus to meet your goals for the day.

A 2 Minute End of Day Recap

At the end of each day, recap your current status, confirm your focus and think about the next day.

Teach this to your employees and improve their productivity as well. Encourage them to stop and ask the same question: *What is the best use of my time right now?* Create a reminder to help trigger the question for you and your employees. Maybe a small, brightly colored Post It note strategically posted in your office. Consider establishing set times during the day such as 11:11 am and 1:11 pm for the time-outs. Or set up a task reminder in Outlook to remind you 3 times a day to re-evaluate your time.

Give it a try for the next 5 work days. Your investment of 65 minutes might just pay off!

Audio Book Short List for Holiday Weekend

Leverage that driving time or flying time this holiday weekend with a good audio book. Here are some books I've recently listened to on my iPhone.

Getting Naked: A Business Fable About Shedding the Three Fears That Sabotage Client Loyalty by Patrick Lencioni. 4 hours 17 minutes. Take Lencioni's perspective to your leadership role and consider how well you are leading with your talents versus leading from scripts and methodologies.

1776 by David McCullough. 6 hours for abridged version. Our country was built on cunningness, determination and great vision. Think you're leading through a difficult transition? Compare notes with some of our early patriots.

Poke the Box by Seth Godin. 2 hours 14 minutes. Rings true with the theme of this Leadership Learning Moment. . . get started, do something, try it, stop waiting for permission.

Divide & Conquer

Overwhelmed in a meeting with a large project? Is an employee struggling with how to get through all the work in front of them?

Use this simplistic project planning tool to help get a handle on the project or work load. Let's use an example: your boss comes to you, asking that you give him a plan to increase employee morale given the recent downsizing at your company.

- Find a blank piece of paper.

- Holding the paper sideways in front of you (landscape mode) fold the paper in half.

- Next, fold the paper in half again.

- Unfold the paper and you'll notice you have 4 quadrants.

- Divide the project at hand into 4 big buckets of work. So for our sample project, we might have the buckets: Employee Morale Issues, Manager Morale Issues, Idea Generation, and Implementing Ideas.

- Within each quadrant begin to develop 3 to 4 smaller buckets of work. So for the Employee Morale Issues quadrant/bucket we might have:

  o Send online survey to employees

  o Gather small groups of employees to seek information

  o Gather small groups of managers to seek perception on employee morale

  o Get materials on what other companies are experiencing with current morale

- Finish all quadrants. Note that neatness doesn't count so use all the space in the quadrant, writing sideways and diagonally as thoughts come to mind.

- Is the work and sub-work in each quadrant still too big? Divide it again, using the back of each quadrant, or take a quadrant to a new piece of paper.

Dividing the project into manageable pieces creates the opportunity to conquer the project at hand, even if the conquering is manipulating your mind to believe the project can be managed.

Are you more visual in your approach? Gather multi-colored post-it notes and a clean wall. Write your buckets of work on the post-its and place them on the wall. Use similar colors for similar themes. Post-it notes allow you to move the items around the wall as your mind rotates through how best to conquer the work ahead. Maybe magic triangles provide a great visual. Or perhaps placing the post-it notes in a logical sequence of implementation. Have some fun with your approach.

You Are What You Eat

A leader is developed over time, just as your body develops. A healthy life style and eating well will produce a healthy body, spirit and outlook. The same can be said for growing your leadership wisdom. Investing time, energy, and focus on your leadership capacity will yield leadership wisdom.

A healthy leadership menu might consist of the following:

- Read any chapter of a current best-selling business book.
- Coach a Little League team.
- Sit in a busy restaurant and study the interactions, conversations and facial expressions of the staff.
- Every day, write down one thing you accomplished during the day that makes you proud of yourself.
- Carve out 15 minutes from your schedule this week for "thinking" time.
- Have lunch with someone who you find difficult to work with.
- Meditate upon and visualize yourself in a successful leadership interaction/event.
- Ask a peer for feedback.
- Volunteer for one hour a month somewhere . . . anywhere.
- Pick a process/team interaction point to analyze this month. How would the CEO assess the item?

Start building your leadership wisdom today!

New Take on Tracking Employee Progress

The depth and breadth of a well prepared performance review is directly proportional to the amount of information you have on the employee for the whole period of time. Tracking employee progress between reviews is something every leader is doing - well, every leader should be doing. The question is always to what extent is the information readily available, which pivots on how you as a leader actually accumulate pertinent employee information over time.

I've been using Evernote, an online content management tool, to manage many aspects of my information management needs. The tool allows me to drive all sorts of information into a database, from directly typing notes to forwarding emails to copying and pasting web-based information. The information can be filtered into notebooks and tagged for easy research.

In particular, I use the notebook's structure to handle each of the executives I coach, allowing me to keep track of our meetings outcomes, agreements on objectives, email updates on activity, etc. I type short notes from my smartphone as well as send emails directly to people's notebooks. At times I find pertinent online tools/articles which I want to use with a certain executive and can directly add those items to the notebooks.

In my experience, leaders too often look back at performance over too short a period of time, losing the perspective of "the trend" of performance, either up or down. I believe the nexus of the problem is the lack of good information to review the activities over time. Maybe you've been great at managing your employee information. If not, maybe a new tool can motivate you to gain ground in this leadership activity.

Huddle up!

Far too many staff meetings are drudgery for attendees, yet these meetings do provide some valuable information. Spice up your staff meetings by changing the dynamics of the meeting through Huddles, a simple, fast and effective meeting format that requires attendees to communicate time-critical information efficiently.

Here are some rules for the Huddle Up meeting:

- Huddles last for 9 minutes.

- Huddles are run standing up. ALL attendees must remain standing for the meeting.

- Pick a unique time of the day that works well with the flow of your team's work. Try one of these times to get started.

  o Start of day: 8:56 am

  o Morning Break: 9:21 am

  o Before Lunch: 11:51 am

  o End of day: 4:41 pm

- Huddle agendas require just 2 items for each participant:

  o What's going on today in your world that will impact others in the room?

  o Is there something specific you need to be successful today?

- Muzzle all electronic devices; everyone – including you – can wait up to 9 minutes to get to that voicemail.

- There's no room for food at the huddle.

You must manage the quick flow of the huddle. While encouraging the give and take of information, be sure to lead your team to develop a cadence for the level of communication that works well. If a more lengthy discussion is needed on a topic, park the topic to be dealt with in a separate meeting at a different location than the huddle.

Here are some ideas to make the huddle even more engaging.

- Use a stuffed animal as the microphone. Have fun passing the stuffed animal around/across the meeting to the next speaker.
- Pick the speaking spot for the room. Rotate the whole group in a circle through the spot, stopping for each participant to speak as needed.
- Hold the meeting in a small space to create a comfortable, crowded feeling.
- Have attendees draw numbers or letters from a hat on the way into the meeting designating their order.

Avoid the E-mail Addiction. Time Block Your Day.

How many emails do you receive on any given day? Formal and informal studies differ on a solid average but the range runs from 48 to 75. The addiction to email is real. You need to immediately respond to the ding or ring indicating a message has arrived. For leaders today, the response is almost Pavlovian.

Take control of your time and focus. Try time blocking your schedule for a day. Decide what times during the day you will review, answer and compose emails. As you plan your day, create three to four 20-minute time blocks which will be dedicated to email. During the remainder of the day turn off your email – all devices and gadgets – removing yourself from the temptation to take a quick read.

During the non-email time, focus on other leadership work at hand. You will likely be amazed at how well you can focus when not being interrupted with the pings, dings and rings of email.

Next question: what to do with the "found time?" Here are a couple of ideas to help you develop your own list.

- Drop by an employee's workstation to have an impromptu, real time, one-on-one, in-person conversation.
- Have lunch with an external peer.
- Take an 18 minute walk to develop an action plan for the next 36 hours.
- Think. Simply use the time to think.

Create and Cultivate Your Peer Network

A leader can often feel quite lonely as the day passes into the evening. The "to do" list is still too long and emails await responses. A recent employee issue weighs heavily on the mind. Tomorrow's calendar is already full with back-to-back meetings.

A network of peer leaders can be tremendously helpful by providing not only keen advice for situational leadership, but a strong sense that you have allies and are not alone in the continual juggle as well. Peer insight and advice can prove to be a strong motivating force for you, as you dig deep into your personal energy bucket.

Set up a schedule to meet with one peer – either in your company or at another company – once per week. Make a rotation of 4 to 5 peers, who you will meet once every 4 to 5 weeks and develop, enrich and cultivate the relationships. In moments of need, reach out to your network for advice, counsel, affirmation, and ideas on managing through a situation. Gain perspective or simply know that you are not alone.

Take Control of Your Time

Time seems to slip by, minutes here, hours there, then suddenly weeks have gone by. As a leader, you have many competing interests for your time during any given day. Current business protocol encourages an endless run at meetings, and at times, it seems you have little control of your destiny. Or can you take control?

Measure It

As you expect your employees to work effectively and efficiently, you should impose the same expectation on yourself. To help get a handle on where the time goes, develop a simple time sheet for a week. Here are some ideas on categories which could be used to delineate your investment of time:

- Others' meetings that were critical
- Meetings I ran that were impactful/important
- Meetings I ran which were less than impactful
- Others' meetings that were not critical
- Talking with my employees
- Emailing/IMing/Texting/On the phone
- Administrative
- Doing work as a working manager
- Thinking time

Take Action

Make a pie chart at the end of the week to help analyze where time was spent. Next, take a look at the data and determine your perspective on the return on the investment of your time for the company and for you as a leader. Develop an action plan based on your assessment of ROI and how you might want to adjust the time.

Learning Moments

Coaching Yourself Up

Learning Moments

Trending Well

As my friend Jerry says, you can have a bad day or bad month or even a bad year. But it's pretty hard to have a bad 5 years. What is important in life is your trend line.

I submit you take a similar approach to your leadership capability. Every one of us has a less than perfect discussion with an employee. And there are days and weeks where we just can't seem to find the right rhythm in leading our teams. Heck, you could have a bad year where you just can't get your department or whole company to be successful.

If you were to map out the components and impacts of your personal leadership capability over several years, do you see a trend line similar to the price of gold over the last 5 years or is your trend line more like that of the value of the housing market?

Here's a hint for you: the measure of your success is not the rise in your income, but in the growth of the asset you are charged with managing.

Permission to Fire

In one of the highly tense scenes in the movie *Top Gun*, the fighter pilot scans his radar screen while working the controls of his fighter jet, trying to line up the crosshairs on the enemy jet he's chasing. The crosshairs align, the screen changes color to red and a loud tone can be heard, followed by the pilot almost yelling "I've got tone. . . I'm going to take the shot. . . Firing."

My good friend, Glenn, has "permission to fire" with me when he's got "tone," meaning he has clarity regarding something in my behavior or thought pattern for which he can provide constructive feedback. We've built a professional and personal friendship to a level where we trust and honor each other and are willing to provide honest, direct feedback. So here's a recent, slightly modified conversation between us.

> Mike: "I had this thing that I didn't follow up on with someone about a year ago."
>
> Glenn: "What was the task, how important was it?"
>
> Mike: "Well, important enough I feel guilty and I still think about not getting to it. I really should have followed through, but I didn't. And I'm not sure why."
>
> Glenn: "OK, I've got tone. Do I have permission to fire?"
>
> Mike: "Come on Glenn, at this point that's a given. Fire away."
>
> Glenn: "It's never too late to do the right thing. Do it today, get it done and move forward."

The power in the feedback comes directly from the allowance of trust and respect in our relationship. That trust wasn't there the first time we met or the fifth time. But along the way, we built a relationship that allows for mutual respect and honesty.

We all need people in our lives with whom we feel so comfortable that almost anything can be said. In the end we must value the feedback and remember that the truth can be our friend.

Take Action

Make a list of your top five colleagues/professional friends. Who on this list should have permission to fire back at you with feedback that can be as direct as needed for the situation? For those who do have permission, take them to lunch and tell them they now have permission to fire when ready at any point in time they get tone.

If you're having trouble thinking of people who can/should have this level of access, you are really limiting your potential as a leader. Consider investing some time in building deeper relationships with a few key people.

Rehire Yourself

Remember those feelings of the first days and weeks in a new job. The thrill of learning a new environment, the freedom from office politics and gossip, the flood of ideas, the intrigue with meeting your employees for the first time, the adrenaline rush of opportunity to make an impact, and the unwavering belief of your boss and peers in your ability to have great success.

Re-create it! Rehire yourself into your position.

Today is your first day of your first week of your first month in the job. Clear your calendar and GTD list (Getting Things Done). Let the fog roll into your memories of relationships.

Start everything anew. . .

- Review your job description
- Re-introduce yourself to your employees
- Craft a vision and align your resources around the vision
- Draw a stakeholder chart of key peers and teams with whom you'll need to establish relationships
- Champion and enable the execution of your plans
- Start a new GTD list

Create the opportunity to allow yourself to be fully motivated for your leadership role. Rehiring yourself will allow your mind to discard old baggage that weighs you down and explore/establish boundaries that enable you to be more effective.

No A**holes Rule

I've become intrigued with a book by Robert Sutton titled *"The No Asshole Rule: Building a Civilized Workplace and Surviving One That Isn't"* which came out in paperback in September 2010. The premise of the book is that organizations bear a huge cost due to the behaviors and impacts of less scrupulous and irritating coworkers and leaders.

Naturally, we all think of ourselves as the good guys/gals in the organization. As such, we are part of the "us" group and not one of "them." But the real question would be how others perceive our behaviors and intentions.

Here's a list of Bob's Dirty Dozen Common Everyday Actions That A**holes Use.

1. Personal insults

2. Invading one's "personal territory"

3. Uninvited physical contact

4. Threats and intimidation, both verbal and nonverbal

5. "Sarcastic jokes" and "teasing" used as insult delivery systems

6. Withering email flames

7. Status slaps intended to humiliate their victims

8. Public shaming or "status degradation" rituals

9. Rude interruptions

10. Two-faced attacks

11. Dirty looks

12. Treating people as if they are invisible

It might be worth your time to take a read through Bob's book and perform a bit of soul searching. Then try seeking some input from those with whom you interact.

38 Days

What can you accomplish in the 38 days?

During 38 days in late 2009, Jacob Shell endured a rare transplant procedure at The Children's Hospital in Boston. As you might know, Jacob Shell, of ShellStrong fame, was 8 years old at the time and had neuroblastoma, a very difficult cancer. During this 38 day journey, Jacob persevered through a 6th round of chemo (more powerful than his first 5 rounds), received his own stem cells through a transplant process and strived through the miraculous rebuilding of his body's immunity. Most of this time he was secluded in a sterile room to help protect his body during the rebuilding of his immunity.

Take inspiration from Jacob's journey. Look at your own performance as a leader and consider how you might benefit from an intensive 38 day treatment procedure.

- **Destroy Bad Habits** – over 7 days, acknowledge and eradicate your bad habits

- **Transplant Day** – in a 3 hour, self-motivated cleansing exercise, transplant a vibrant outlook unto yourself; feel the inflow of your talents and abilities and happiness

- **Re-build** – Every day for 30 days begin one healthy habit, skill, phrase to repeat, relationship, thought, action, task

Start tomorrow, or Monday, or Wednesday. Count out 38 days on your calendar and on that day take account of how your professional and personal lives are progressing.

Keep a healthy perspective during your journey. Jacob was fighting for his life. You're just fighting for happiness and success.

How's the Street View

Have you used Google Maps Street View in the past? What a great way to drop in and see the actual destination of your trip. You can see the building, street, and parking, even what restaurants might be close by.

A professional roadmap helps you to document where you'd like to head in the future, prompting you to develop a target, areas of focus, goals and broad actions to lay out your professional trip. Maybe you're just taking a small trip to expand your skills a bit, or possibly a once in a lifetime, cross-country trip, taking you on a 2-year adventure to reach that next rung in the ladder.

You should check in on your progress, just as Google Maps lets you drill down from a broad, global view to the street view.

Regional View – you can see your starting point, your ending point and the organizational terrain you'll cross.

Neighborhood View – you can see more details regarding bends in the road, turns that will need to be made, special navigational opportunities (shortcuts, country roads, highways), all with pros and cons.

Street View – The real deal! What is actually around you at the moment in time when the snapshot is taken?

To Think About

- Where are you on your roadmap?

- Is the highway really your best choice or might the country road with all its scenery build more leadership wisdom?

- What feedback might a passer-by at street level be able to provide?

Swimming Blind

Michael Phelps won the 200-meter butterfly in the 2008 Olympics by seven-tenths of a second and set a world record, while swimming blind. The last 100 meters of the race, his goggles filled with water. He had practiced his race so many times *in his mind,* seeing every action, every movement, and every breath while playing the mental video of the race every day, that he didn't miss a stroke when his water-filled goggles blinded him. The practice in the pool and in his mind allowed him to see the final race before he swam it.

A leader's role in delivering feedback is not about the employee's perception of self as much as it is about the leader's wisdom as he looks upon the behaviors exhibited by the employee, and sees opportunities for growth. Sharing that wisdom creates the opportunity for the employee to truly grow. It is critically important that a leader understands the wisdom he can share AND more importantly, be ready and able to communicate that wisdom in perfect fashion. Regardless of how deep their wisdom may be, great leaders are effective, inspirational, and impactful because they know how best to deliver the feedback.

Preparing to deliver key messages requires practice, and practicing like Michael Phelps can make you better. Great leaders know that "you need to see it before you do it," meaning that practicing the delivery of feedback messages will create the opportunity to refine and perfect the delivery. Practicing the delivery requires repeating feedback phrases/sound bites, allowing you to adjust the tone and inflection to determine the best way to package the content to be heard. Seeing in your mind how employees will receive the various forms of messages provides the behavioral repetition that can be called upon when needed.

When it's game time and you're called upon to deliver that critical feedback message with wisdom, will you be ready? Will you have practiced enough? Repeat after me: *See it before you do it.*

Surround Yourself with Positive Leaders

We've all seen him, that leader who just has a black cloud hovering over his head throughout the day. The world seems dark around him. He is unhappy with the changes in direction of the company, changes that were announced 7 months ago. He's discouraged with his team that appears to always be in some type crisis, and he spreads gossip about other leaders.

Every day you have a choice regarding how you will approach the day. Dr. Norman Vincent Peale's *Power of Positive Thinking* provides great insight on the power of your perspective. The day will be what you perceive the day to be. Surrounding yourself with positive-minded leaders will create an atmosphere that inspires you to approach the day's challenges with a strength, an inspiration to be the best leader you can be. Surround yourself with negative leaders and the opposite will likely happen. The day will be fraught with insurmountable problems, constant headaches and discontent among the people.

Take a moment to read each statement below. Which one of these statements best describes your perspective today, as others will perceive you?

1. **Leading is a lonely job.** Today is filled with more meetings, listening to my team tell me why their work is behind schedule. Then I'll have to listen to someone complain about his continuing problems with a co-worker. And to boot, I have to sit through a 2-hour status meeting over lunch.

2. **Leading is such a great job.** I have the fantastic opportunity to inspire, grow, and motivate people. I look forward to the challenge today of helping someone feel great about her work. The guidance I will provide will be thoughtful, have impact and help my organization to achieve success today. During the status meeting today, I'm going to sit in a

different seat and learn one new thing from the person next to me.

Life's short. Find the positive leaders with whom you can mingle. Be inspired; be inspiring to others. It's your choice to make.

The List

See if you can answer these questions.

1. What team won the last Super Bowl? Name the last 5 Super Bowl winning teams.

2. Who won on last season's Survivor reality TV show? Who were the last 5 winners?

3. What team won the World Series this year? Name the last 5 World Series winners.

4. Who won the Grammy for Best Female Country Vocal Performance in 2011? Who were the last 5 winners?

5. Which TV Comedy Series won the Golden Globe Award earlier this year for that category? What shows won for the last 5 years?

6. Who were/are the 5 people who most impacted your professional life?

My guess is that you may have been able to get some answers to questions 1 through 5, especially the most recent winner, but you were likely challenged with remembering the last 5 winners. But how did you do with question #6? Most people can quickly come up with 5 people who had a direct and substantial impact on their professional lives. The mentoring, guidance, patience, support, wisdom provided were the building blocks to how you act and behave in your leadership role. What they told you, and more importantly, how they acted and behaved, taught you how you can be successful.

Take Action

Quickly, make a list of those 5 people. Invest one minute on each person, capturing what you learned from each. Take 2 minutes in a power pose (feet up on desk, hands behind the head) and ponder the value of the wisdom you have gained from those folks on your list.

Now, ask yourself: If your employees were asked the same series of questions above, would your name be on their list in #6?

Leadership Nirvana

Vince Lombardi, the great football coach, taught his players to "run with complete abandon, and when you get close to the goal, let nothing stop you from getting across."

Do you believe in your management and leadership skills to a point where you can honestly lead with complete abandon and lead your team to achieve its goals? What can you do today to fully believe that you can lead your team to great success?

In most self-help books, a common theme is utilized wherein you need to visualize your successful state in order to realize success. While the books, tapes, and programs differ in how they want to help you obtain this state of nirvana, maybe leadership nirvana in our case, it is evident that pushing yourself to believe that you are a successful leader will help you to be a successful leader.

Start today. . .

- **Repeat to yourself** 10 times that you are a _____ leader. Fill in the blank with a word that best describes your leadership nirvana. Here are some suggestions: successful, compassionate, dynamic, consistent, communicative, stable, change agent, patient, strong.

- **Hit the bookstore** – or your bookcase, for a motivating self-help book, tape, or program. Amazon has no less than 100,765 Self Help and 360,712 Motivation books in its list. Need a recommendation? Here are several from my bookcase:

  o *The Power of Positive Thinking* by Dr. Norman Vincent Peale

  o *The Last Lecture* by Randy Pausch

  o *Poke the Box* by Seth Godin

- Commit to it. Tell a colleague, a friend, or a significant other that you are going to spend the next four weeks focusing on being a more successful leader. Ask them to follow up with you to see how it's going.

- Spend 22 minutes writing your *Jerry Maguire* mission statement.

You can take action and let nothing stand in your way of reaching the goal line or you can choose to accept mediocrity.

I'm a Great Leader

How are you measuring your success and effectiveness as a leader? What scale is used? To whom are you comparing yourself?

A friend of mine was more than happy to talk about his glory days as a distinguished athlete at his school. He was a starter on varsity teams all three seasons of the school year for several years. While he was proud of his success, he was self-actualized enough to also reveal his balanced perspective in that he was successful in a school that was rather small when compared to most. He understood that the ruler used to measure the perception of his success differed, depending upon the environment.

The ruler that measures your success as a leader can change over time. It seems critically important that you be clairvoyant in determining which rulers you will use at what times. You may very well be the best leader in your company. But if you company is full of "leadership challenged executives," exactly what level of success are you really enjoying?

Questions to ponder:

- To whom or what am I comparing myself to as a leader?

- How would I perceive my leadership effectiveness if I was at XYZ company?

HR: Friend or Foe?

Human Resources professionals are there to help you. Though it might not look that way at all times, HR knows that the relative strength of their leaders corresponds directly to the number of people problems they will or won't have. The primary function of HR is to build the talent capacity within the organization through the acquisition of talented new hires and the internal development of talented employees. Unfortunately, HR is also responsible for cleaning up the messes that so many less-than-talented leaders create.

Most of your interactions with HR will revolve around employee-specific events: hiring, reviews, promotions, salary actions, or firings. In some ways HR is like your auto mechanic. You usually visit the mechanic only when there's a problem with your car. You're not happy about the inconvenience and the need to juggle your schedule to deal with the situation. When you get the call from the mechanic regarding his analysis of the situation, it's usually bad/painful news which will cost you money, time and energy.

The mechanic will likely tell you that if you had been bringing your car in for oil changes and routine maintenance, then this problem would likely not have surfaced. Or, he could have caught the problem earlier and fixed it at a lower cost and/or impact to you.

So how can you better work with the HR staff on preventive maintenance of your staff?

- Ask for a meeting to discuss your current analysis of your team and your development plans for your employees.

- Every quarter, meet with HR regarding your views of the interactions of your team and its performance levels, as well as your ongoing performance discussions.

- Seek a meeting with the highest level HR person with whom you could meet. Ask for informal feedback from the HR leader on how he/she perceives your leadership capability in the organization.

- Ask HR to shadow several of your staff meetings and then debrief you regarding their observations.

- Send an email or voice mail to HR regarding something good that happened with an employee. The positive news will be much appreciated.

Take some time to walk in the shoes of the HR professional. The perspective might help you to strengthen your leadership wisdom and improve your relationship with HR.

Quit to Win

Steve Jobs was a grand quitter. While he was immensely successful building and running Apple, he strategically leveraged quitting. He quit acclaimed Reed College after one semester and decided working at then wildly famous Atari wasn't as important as back-packing around India. What is intriguing is that Steve Jobs quit to win.

When can quitting – stopping a project, stopping pursuit of the next promotion, leaving a job – be a successful strategic decision?

As a leader, you are consistently challenged with how to best allocate limited resources against projects, special initiatives, and normal work. What may be key to your decision-making is how you massage the economic theories behind the art of your decisions, which are based on sunk costs (what's already been expended) and opportunity costs (the potential return on the use of the resource).

The authors of *Freakonomics** (books, blogs, radio, and website) have some interesting perspective on the **virtues** of quitting in a recent podcast of a PBS radio interview on the topic. Invest 6 minutes to take a listen and gain some perspective on your career and leadership potential/impact.

To Think About – When in your life/career has quitting been successful? And alternatively, when in your life/career would quitting have been the better choice?

*http://www.freakonomics.com/2011/06/29/quitting-time/

Adjust Your Paradigm: Fire Yourself

We all can get caught up in our self-perception regarding how important we are in our leadership roles, as well as the effectiveness we enable within our organization as fairly decent leaders. Leadership effectiveness is dependent upon your capability to leverage relationships to achieve goals. The depth and breadth of these professional relationships depend heavily on the level of activity you invest in them.

I find many executives limit their investment in building and sustaining the quality of professional relationships within their current organization and, as importantly, outside their organization. They are with colleagues in meetings all the time, but there is little investment in building the quality of those relationships.

Take 15 minutes to fire yourself and review your relationships.

- Quickly, handwrite a 2 sentence memo firing yourself.

- Make a list of the 20 people you would contact to let them know about your transition.

- Make note of when was the last time you had real contact with each of these 20 people, with contact defined as meeting for lunch, dinner, coffee or a phone conversation.

- Make a list of who within your current organization could – and would – provide a recommendation on your leadership capability.

- Assess your LinkedIn profile. How many contacts do you maintain? How up-to-date is your profile?

The paradigm exploration you should seek is to inventory your relationships, taking note of whom you should be investing time with to make sure you're in tune with their professional and personal lives. It's likely that the converse will be true and they will be in tune with your life. Now, imagine if you had their real time perspective/advice/input on your leadership challenges.

Take Action

Ask yourself: Am I willing to commit to meet with one person a week over the next 20 weeks to increase the depth and breadth of my relationships and gain perspective on the growth of my leadership capability?

Functional Leadership Complacency

Are you a leader or a functional leader? Companies expect leaders to be generally strong at leading others and specifically strong at leading functions. Unfortunately many leaders grow up within specific business functions, gaining experience and greater levels of authority. The scope of responsibility is a combination of people leadership and technical mastery. And when these leaders hit the ripe age of their mid-40s, they have successfully prepared themselves to become complacent with leading. They know the ins and outs of the business function and adequately lead their areas, but lack a depth of curiosity and passion for actual leadership. So they have a tendency to go on an auto pilot of sorts.

Think about the leaders of finance, IT, human resources, operations, sales. They are recruited and groomed because they have deep functional expertise. Now think about the really great leaders you have known or read about. Most often, these leaders gained experience and wisdom through diverse leadership experiences. This diversity allows multiple lenses to be used when viewing and assessing situations, strategies, and solutions.

Ponder This: You have been asked to lead a business function or team that is completely outside your functional knowledge base. Maybe you're an HR leader being asked to run finance, or a sales leader being asked to run IT. How exactly would you lead this group? How would you establish the goals, how would you make timely decisions, what methods and tools would you utilize to understand the momentum of the group? And maybe the most important question: How much time would you invest in knowing and trusting the people you lead?

What CEOs Have To Say

Recently, I had the opportunity to moderate an armchair discussion between two CEOs for an audience of HR executives. Not surprisingly, a predominant theme during the discussion focused on leadership. Here's a rundown of some of the salient take-aways from these two CEOs regarding what they look for in leaders.

- **Read. . . A Lot** – Great leaders are prolific readers. Not only journals in their specialty areas or just business books. They read books that interest them and provide broad exposure to stimulate the mind. They read, or re-read: classics, fiction, non-fiction, and mysteries. Creative problem solving starts with diverse thinking.

- **Liberal Arts Degrees** – They look for those people who have been taught to think critically, research deeply, and have broad exposure to knowledge.

- **Divergent Backgrounds** – Combinations of degrees and experience that are not strictly an ascension of specialty education. An MBA in Finance to balance the functional expertise in technology or HR. The career progression that reveals leadership work in operational, staff, and customers arenas.

- **Networking** – Network upwards and backwards. Seek long-term connection with and insight from people who are two levels above your current role. Stay in contact with professors who can provide specialty insight and are often happy to be asked.

- **Respect** – Respectfulness of seasoned employees and leaders who have built the sustenance of the company. Respect for the culture.

- **Want to Be Here** – We want to have leaders – and employees as well – who **want** to be at the company, not feel they are bound to the company.

The great art of leadership comes from investing the time to feed the brain, to connect the dots of the future, and ultimately guide your team to the place they will need to be in the future when those dots connect in the real world.

Have Heart

Great managers execute well and help their teams to deliver on the organization's priorities. Hard working employees will deliver for great managers.

Great leaders have heart and create passion for a cause. Passionate employees will give all they have to assure success of a cause.

Find your heart and evolve into a great leader.

I Start Stuff

How do you respond to the phrase, "tell me about yourself?" Common answers include your job title, your scope of responsibility, the magnitude of power you yield and maybe a small piece of data on your personal life. Interestingly, as we at look how leaders typically spend their days, it becomes evident that most spend their time holding or attending meetings, scanning a hundred emails without reading them, fitting into the culture, or appeasing those more powerful and attempting to stay the course for the ever- changing goals.

Seth Godin, in his book, *Poke the Box*, challenged that most people just follow. They don't start; they don't initiate or instigate. We're not rewarded for starting and failing but we are rewarded for fitting in and following the mandate.

We're trained to fit in, seek security, and hold back creativity and there is great fear and anxiety of standing out. Seth's perspective: anxiety is experiencing failure in advance. Let that sink in and really think about that concept. When did you last experience anxiety?

"The simple thing that separates successful individuals from those who languish is the very thing that separates exciting and growing organizations from those that stagnate and die. The winners turn initiative into a passion and a practice. . . The challenge is getting into the habit of starting." Seth Godin

Start something today for you and for those you think are following you:

- Make a list of things you could've started but haven't.

- Watch a 3 minute video of Seth Godin talking about his book and The Domino Project.

- Invest 10 minutes to scan the workbook Seth's group created.

- Buy – and read or listen to – his book.

Worst Cooks in Your Organization

I love the reality show, *Worst Cooks in America*. Self-select yourself into a process that starts with saying "Hey, I'm terrible at this" and be willing to learn in front of the world. The cooks start at square one, learning the art and science of proper vegetable-cutting techniques, and then their training builds up from there. What a humbling experience.

It would be great if organizations – and those who lead organizations – had the guts to create an atmosphere and culture wherein low performing leaders would have the confidence to self-select into a program that starts with the same premise: Hey, I'm terrible at leadership. Visualize it . . . a room full of leaders, ranging from a couple of directors, to some managers, several supervisors, and a whole bunch of VPs, all admitting they are in over their heads in this leadership thing. All of them ready to learn how to be the best leader they could be.

Or maybe the visualization is an organization excelling at achieving its goals, a population of employees and leaders who are energized with their jobs and a culture of growth.

The Shallow Leader

What makes leaders great? They know *why* they lead. Seems simple really, that if you truly know your purpose in leading and the value system which resonates those beliefs, then your behaviors will reveal your leadership principles. The difficulty for many leaders is that their "why" of leading is shallow. They are doing the activities leaders are supposed to do and they are acting in ways leaders are supposed to act, but they lack the breadth and depth of the "why.

Think about it. . . Are you leading people because you truly want to guide them? Or are you leading others for the money? Is it for the prestige? Because it was the next logical step? For the power?

Walk carefully in your leadership role, because the shallowness of your intent – the why factor – may just bleed through.

Who's The Adult In The Room

Managing employees is a lot like raising kids and someone has to be the adult in the room. Best bet is you're being paid to be that person. Employees and kids need the following. . .

- Boundaries of appropriate performance and behavior

- Guiding advice and latitude to make character-building mistakes

- Care and feeding

- Deadlines and curfews

- Follow- up to see if they accomplished what they said they'd accomplish

- Affection, recognition, counsel and every now and then a hug

A good leader will develop wisdom over time that will allow her to provide just the right amount of freedom and restriction to motivate and inspire her employees as each employee grows and develops. A key insight is to know the "work age" of your employees, and subsequently, the appropriate levels of freedom and restriction. Here's a start to a list describing the age of employees.

- **Toddler** – curious, desires immediate feedback, will work until he drops, temper tantrum when he doesn't get his way, desires love and affection to know you care

- **Tweener** – intrigued, works diligently but easily distracted with technology, trying to fit in to the culture, likes attention but maybe not in public

- **Teenager** – works independently but wants to know there are some restrictions, rebellious to autocratic power, can be lazy at times, inclusion, caring though not reciprocated

- **College Aged** – passion for causes, works odd hours and will work endlessly if motivated, out-of-the-box thinking as knowledge and wisdom converge, seeks equal but separate relationships

List your employees and label their current age. Now, think through various transactions and events with each employee, assuming their work age and the success or struggles you're having with each. How are you performing? Are you building up your employees to be successful in society? And most importantly, are you being a "parent" or attempting to be a friend?

Be Honorable

There are times in your life as a leader when you will need to make a decision regarding doing the right thing, and treating people the right way. We could discuss the pros and cons with various approaches to doing the right thing and the varied scales of defining right, and while the subjectivity of defining right is understandable at some point, the definition is not an intellectual exercise. You will be forced to decide how you will act.

For some leaders this moment in time comes as they've developed realignment plans for the organization and those plans include an impact on employees. While many difficult decisions must be made to balance the financial aspects of the impact, there is a right and honorable way in which to deal with the employees. Transition money will be important to the impacted employees but the belief that they were treated in a professional, dignified and humanistic manner through an incredibly difficult process is ultimately more important.

Act honorably and have the courage to do the right thing.

Be Selfish – Take a Mini-Retreat.

Investing in your own development can reap tremendous rewards. Invigorate your effectiveness by taking a personal offsite day. Set up an agenda for the day that includes an inventory of what has been working, revisiting your goals, assessing the perception of stakeholders of your team's work, dreaming about what could be accomplished and making executable action plans.

Determine a location where you can truly relax, reflect and plan. Consider these ideas.

- Grab a hotel room about an hour's drive away, providing just enough distance to feel as if you have traveled to the offsite and giving you the buffer from easy access to your office.

- Pick a state park, pack a lunch and find a picnic table to spread out on.

- Rent a boat and float in the middle of the lake for 4 hours.

- Take a train ride to a city 3 hours away and stay on the train for the round trip.

- Do you prefer to have people and noise around? How about driving to a college campus and using the school's student union, café or library.

- Prefer to add in some food? Panera Bread probably has a location in every major city. Take a 60 minute drive and park yourself at Panera.

- Is money an issue? How about a friend's house? Using a known environment for a different purpose might just provide the fresh perspective to invigorate your thinking.

Take 20 minutes now and make a plan for your personal mini-retreat.

82

Seeking Authentic Leadership

We know authentic leadership when we see it and at times when it is absent. Authenticity, that genuine, honorable, right stuff that is revealed as leaders walk forward ahead of their teams, behaving in ways which portray the culture they believe can be built.

We teach managers to become leaders through adaptation of behaviors and development of key skills. But authenticity is difficult, if not impossible to teach. We often look to rules, policies, laws, and regulations to guide behavior and instill a sense of expectations for situations in which leaders may find themselves. Leaders grow up following the organizational and societal structures which enable them to effectively lead within the organizations and industries they have chosen. We understand that the banking executive's environment is much different than that of a software executive and still different from that of a hotel executive.

But there is a higher standard that cannot be found in law or a policy or a handbook or Robert's Rules of Order. There is a standard to which, in my opinion, all leaders should judge themselves. The standard of what's appropriate, what's the right thing to do when the rule book just doesn't go far enough in detailing every imaginable scenario. The standard that demands the leader make non-selfish decisions and put the good of employees – individually and in total – ahead of self-interests.

Now is an opportune time to assess whether you been an authentic leader or a selfish leader. I recommend you invest an hour reviewing your decisions, and the trend line of your actions through the last 12 months. Think through your motivations and rationalizations for decisions and conversations. Worried about investing a whole hour? Maybe that worry is a good place to start your assessment.

Change Your View: Drive a New Route Home Today

We challenge ourselves each and every day to achieve. Problems arise and we solve them. Employees have issues and we deal with them. As a leader, you expend a great deal of energy to creatively solve small and big problems. At times you'll find your energy level to be low, which should alert you to a need to refuel the energy. Studies have shown that minor shifts in your perspective can provide a great deal of impact in solving problems. New perspectives can be gained from the simplest of changes to your daily routine. Buy your morning coffee at a different shop. Park in a different section of the parking lot. Take a walk at lunch. Take a different seat in the staff meeting.

As you commute home today, take a different route. For those who drive, take the back roads home instead of the interstate or take a route through a different section of town. Using public transportation? Take a different train or bus. On the train, move further down the platform to sit in a different car. On the bus take a different seat. Sit if you stand or stand if you sit. Changing the scenery can provide a small spark to challenge your creativity.

Create variety in your habits and you'll likely find variety and energy in your problem solving.

Communications

Learning Moments

Unfiltered, Uncensored, Direct Feedback

Remember the movie, *What Women Want* with Mel Gibson? The actor plays a chauvinistic executive who gains an ability to hear what women are actually thinking. He's amazed, intrigued, and ultimately horrified at what women are really thinking about him. How powerful would you find the ability to hear what your employees really think about you, your management style, and your communication style? Imagine unfiltered, uncensored, direct feedback.

Well, we can't make that magic happen in real life. But we can help you think through how "you" perceive your management communication style. Think through the words below with respect to how you perceive your management style. Force rank the words, with the first word being the most like your style, and last word being the least like your style.

Action	Drive
Encouragement	Collaboration
Objectivity	Challenge
Support	Reliability

Too tough to force rank those style words? Then pick the two that best describe your management communication style.

To Think About

Using the work above, think through how your management style mixes with the natural communication styles of your employees. Sugar and water? Oil and water? Somewhere in between? Want to see a sample of a manager's self-assessment? Check out our website to see a sample *Everything* **DiSC**® *Management* profile.

DiSC® *is a registered trademark of Inscape Publishing, Inc.*

Cultural Storytelling

My friend Jerry can tell a heck of a story. He pulls in that southern charm, teases you with just enough data to paint the picture in your head and then delivers the guts of the story. In a matter of 3 to 4 minutes, he has conveyed a full set of moral values, usually with a laugh that can bring you to tears.

For your organization a good story can reveal so much about the culture of the organization. The blending of experiences, people, events, success, challenge, tragedy, and life converge within the organization over time to create the existing culture. Great leaders work hard to build a culture they believe will allow the organization to survive and excel over time. These leaders know that culture, good and bad, evolves over time, and well told stories reveal the threads of people and events that created desired aspects of the culture. The leaders use the stories and history to paint the picture of the desired cultural state.

As you daydream in one of your back-to-back meetings today, meditate on the phrase "cultural storytelling." What messages, morals, history, and behaviors would you like to convey to employees the next time you tell a story from the old or not so old days?

WikiLeaks: Next Up, Your Emails!

I've been pondering how American Diplomats are assessing their exposure, given the forced transparency of some of their secret cables via the WikiLeaks cable dumping. Are they embarrassed? Worried? Fearful? Relieved? Anxious? Distraught? I imagine that each individual is wondering how others view their integrity as compared to the perception of that integrity, pre-WikiLeaksCablegate.

What if all the emails, text messages and voice mails you've sent to your boss (es) and peers were suddenly available for all your employees and friends to view, analyze and decipher? Would your integrity be questioned or diminished? In what ways would your capability to lead be impacted?

Trustworthiness, integrity and credibility are great descriptors of good leadership. But the origin of these qualities ultimately comes from your values, and the alignment of those values with your behavior reveals the core truth about you. And that truth is always present, even if hidden by the supposed veil of secrecy.

Climbing the Communication Stairway

Listening is one of those skills we learned early in life. We've "refined" the skill over time, but maybe the refinement has been more of filter management than enhancement of skills. Here are some possible reasons as to why we're not good listeners.

- It's difficult to put aside our own self-interest
- The speaking/comprehension gap
- No training or focused practice
- We just don't care

Set a goal to build your level of communication and climb the communication stairway.

Level #1: Listener's response ignores speaker's message – Not listening

Level #2: Listener's response reflects his own message – shifts to telling "his story."

Level #3: Listener's response indicates surface understanding, but may minimize speaker's feelings or intended message – judges, agrees or disagrees

Level #4: Listener's response indicates surface understanding – listening for how message impacts self – "what I need to do with the information"

Level #5: Listener's response indicates deeper understanding, helping the speaker to further express or clarify himself – hearing beyond the word – listening for understanding.

Depending on the situation, we need to engage in a different level of listening.

Why You Make So Much Money

Question to Ponder: Why have organizations invested such large sums of money to fund supervisors, team leaders, managers, project managers, regional managers, associate directors, directors, senior directors, VPs, senior VPs, CFOs, CAOs, CIOs, COOs, and CEOs?

A very intriguing theme from the book *Smart Swarm* was the ability of mere insects – ants, bees, termites – to architect amazingly complex homes/factories without the need of a leader. Locating, constructing, operating, fixing, and protecting their factories was all accomplished without the need to have a hierarchy of leadership and dutiful managers. An important key to the success of these insects turns out to be the unique methods of communication that have been adapted over time.

Companies invest those large sums of money in people like you in the hope that you will enable effective communication within, among and at times in spite of the team or organization. The ideal result is motivated and productive, dynamic humans who together can accomplish goals to increase corporate, societal and/or cultural wealth. You are the short-term solution until we evolve our unique methods of communication.

By the way, the insects have been evolving for over 100 million years, so your professional leadership role isn't going away soon, assuming of course that your ROI is trending well.

Keep the Conversation Going

Have regular conversations with your employees, one-on-one, about their work and themselves. It shows your employees you are interested and care about meeting their needs. The information you learn will help you to better manage each person and you will find that your employees will appreciate the conversation.

Below are some questions you can consider asking. Keep in mind however, you shouldn't ask them all at once. Just "sprinkle" them from time to time as you meet with an employee or as you are having a conversation. Be sincere in your approach and remember that your response, both verbal and non-verbal, will determine how much information the person is willing to share. So listen carefully, don't judge, query further, and follow up as needed.

- Do you get enough regular, candid feedback? What additional feedback would you like? Do you have any thoughts on what type of feedback is most helpful to you?

- Do you feel recognized for your accomplishments? Tell me about work you've done that went "unnoticed." I want to know what I'm missing.

- Do you feel your job matches your skills and interests?

- Are you challenged in your day-to-day work?

- Is the training you want available to you?

- Would you like to develop a career plan? Do you need assistance?

- What are you struggling with?

- What would make your work and life easier?

- What makes you want to stay here? What will keep you here on a long-term basis?

- What might lure you away?

- How does this job meet your needs? How does this job not meet your needs?

- What do you like best about your job? Least?

- What do you like best about working here? Least?

- What do I do that is helpful for you? What do I do that is not helpful? What could I do differently?

The rewards of keeping the lines of communication open with your employees will be many.

Don't guess – Ask

Managers sometimes wonder, what motivates my employees, what satisfies them, what will make the biggest difference to an employee? Sometimes we make the mistake of assuming that the same thing motivates all employees: a new assignment, recognition, a promotion. But what motivates a person is likely to be as individual as that person is himself.

So how do you find out? Ask. Talk – a real, live conversation – with each employee about what satisfies him, what they like and dislike about their job, what motivates them personally and professionally. Your goal is to get to know the individual and respond accordingly. Your success in managing each person is largely dependent upon how well you get to know each person and what drives him. So strike up some conversations, ask some questions and listen to the answers. It's likely that just the process of your asking will have a positive impact as well – it will show you're interested and that you care – something most everyone is motivated by!

Make a list today of your employees and a goal date by which you will have a conversation regarding what motivates them. Create a list of questions and conversation starters that will help you to get to the real question on motivation.

Black Hole Leadership. . . Not a Best Practice

Emails. . . performance reviews. . . status reports. . . draft PowerPoint presentations. . . last week's metrics. . . information from the senior leadership update. Are you the tollgate, stopping the flow of information and decisions to your team? Or are you becoming a black hole – all energy being pulled in and collapsing under the weight of non-decisive leadership?

Avoid this trap. Determine your areas of weakness that may create inappropriate tollgates to the abyss.

Email – Do people send you e-mails that you don't respond to? If someone sent you a message, beyond an FYI, it is likely they are looking for a response. When you don't respond, their frustration builds and progress slows. Develop good response habits. Briefly acknowledge the message. Even a "got it" lets someone know that what they've shared is on your radar screen. If you are regularly getting messages that you shouldn't, take the time to let people know how you would like things handled instead.

Build Empowerment – Aid progress by letting people know that if you don't respond to their email or call, they are empowered to move forward without you, or that they are welcome to bug you again without repercussion. Create a default turnaround time of X days on informational reports. No response means all is good.

Do as I Do, not as I Say – Reveal the behavior you expect in others. Performance reviews are as important as their timeliness. They do have a "best used by date" that employees live to. That PowerPoint review/revision process should be within 24 hours.

Key Information from Senior Leadership – Must be timely, which means you are already late in delivering the information. Are there CNN headlines or sound bites that can be sent out in quick bullets? Can you forward along the notes ahead of your weekly status meeting? If you need to cultivate the message and delivery is critical, then make sure that you deliver the information in short order.

Be careful. If you are a black hole, there could be something nasty looming on the other side!

Letting Employees Know You Know

Employees want to know that you, as their leader, are in tune with their progress against their goals. Their innate desire is to receive attention, but the attention must be in forms they prefer whenever possible. As you look at your team of direct reports, think about how each one prefers to receive attention and adjust your information flow and tracking to match those styles.

- The domineering employee will likely want to be given 2 to 3 highlights of what she is working on.

- The conscientious employee will want you to know the due dates and specific themes of his primary tasks or work load.

- The social butterfly will want you to convey how well he is collaborating with his teammates.

- The consistent, consensus employee will want you to understand how her workload is impacting her in comparison to others.

Use your instincts or formal assessment tools to gather intelligence regarding how your employees like to interact with their environment. Then find ways to adjust your style to better match theirs.

Learning Moments

Developing Talent

Learning Moments

How Hiring is Like Storage Wars

The show, *Storage Wars* on A&E, provides a look into the world of modern day archeologists seeking treasures buried in storage units that have been forfeited due to nonpayment. Potential bidders for the auction have the opportunity to look through the door of the storage unit for a couple of minutes, but they cannot touch anything in the unit. Peering in on the stacks and piles, the bidders must discern what treasures may be buried within the unit, using their wisdom, insight, and instincts.

When interviewing a candidate and making a hiring decision, we're no better off than the bidders on Storage Wars. We get some perspective, a glimpse of the real person, as we dig through their credentials, talk to references and work through the interview circuit. But we can't truly see the whole person, how they will interact with our culture or how they will deploy their experience and ambition.

It's been said that you see the best of an employee during the interview, so you're gambling that the reality won't be too far removed from what you've found during the interview process. But sometimes, every now and then, you do make an extraordinary hire. You find that diamond in the rough. Like the bidder on *Storage Wars* who finds the diamond ring buried in the shoebox inside the old duffle bag and smiles at the reality of finding a treasure worth 100 times what they paid for the storage unit. This diamond for you is realizing that you've not only invested in a successful employee, but found a future leader whose rippling positive impact will be felt across employees, customers and vendors for decades to come.

Get Inspired: Watch a previous *Storage Wars* show online. Think through how the show, the bidders, and the storage units parallel your work environment, the team you lead, and your leadership behaviors.

The Sky is Falling

The sky is falling and you have yet another staff meeting at 1:00. The USA is in a recession, the markets are falling, or rising to fall yet again, budgets are being reviewed/cut, and layoffs are being announced. Once-venerable companies teeter on the sharp edge of bankruptcy or engulfment by a competitor, only to be remembered in an MBA case study in the near future.

A structural shift in the economy – local, state, country, global – is impacting all businesses. What are you doing to structurally shift your management priorities and style to be prepared to take advantage of the opportunities that may exist? YES, there are opportunities. Who among your peers has successfully managed a business function, or business, through the forthcoming changes?

This is fertile ground for leaders to show their stuff and build new organizational management techniques. Now is the time when good leaders become great leaders by running on instincts, leveraging solid management techniques and testing new techniques. The core competencies of your business function or team you lead will become clearly evident as traumatic events ripple through your organization. Good leaders will seek this shift in status quo to see the business function's core competencies and talented resources in new ways.

You need to invest time now, today, to think through your resource capacity, workflow constraints, and capabilities. Here are some thought-provoking questions/statements to get you started.

- Your budget is being cut in half. How will you allocate your resources in the most efficient and effective way? Where is your true talent within the team?

- If only 40% of the work that flows through your department, business function or business will be there in the future, describe the work that will remain. Answer the who, what, where, when and how of the work.

- Make a confidential list today of your staff, force ranking them along 3 scales:

    1. General performance measures from the past year

    2. Nimbleness – capacity and ability to adapt

    3. Survivability Factor – talent/ability/skills/energy that could be necessary for the company to continue as a viable entity

- What talent would I acquire from a competitor that isn't as nimble?

- What policies, procedures, bureaucracy are non-critical in our new world?

Which Lens Are You Using Today?

The successful performance in a role by someone who reports to you is based more on your perception of his or her performance than the actual work delivered. Technically, you have cognitive bias in the way you see traits, characteristics, and behaviors, which creates a halo of perception with regard to performance.

Practically speaking: Your perception is driven by which lens you choose to use.

- Your **positive lens** filters your perception of performance with a beam of warmth like a bright spring morning. Those little problems or mistakes do muck up progress but no one can be perfect all the time. And growth comes with learning from mistakes and gaining wisdom.

- Your **negative lens** filters your perception of performance with a negative fog that envelopes your view of work being performed. Every step, every task, every interaction, and every project seems to be less than satisfactory.

A difficult wisdom-building step for leaders is gaining the capability to ascertain the exact moment in time when the tipping point occurs in your frustration with an individual's performance and you decide to change the lens from warmth to fog. Most leaders just seem to find themselves past the point of no return with fog engulfing the view of performance for an employee and anything she does never quite measures up. A self-fulfilling prophesy, (a declared truth which is actually false, but influences/confuses people regarding the behavior that ultimately fulfills the once-false prophecy) will undoubtedly play out and the employee will quickly find himself on the back end of a performance improvement plan.

To Think About

- Have you been a good leader without bias while perceiving performance of those you are charged to lead? Were you performing at 100% in your role? Were you wearing the correct lens?

- Do you consciously decide when to place on the appropriate lens?

- Are you truly perceiving performance or is your vision a bit blurry? Are you nearsighted? Farsighted?

- On a personal level, when in your life have you been basking in the sunshine and warmth or the desolation of the fog? Was the perception of your performance accurate?

Seven Areas to Enable Performance

For an employee to perform well, there are seven areas of need that must be met.

- Knowledge and skill
- Capacity
- Clear expectations
- Defined standards and measures
- Proper conditions
- Incentives
- Feedback

When an employee isn't performing well, we too often assume it's a "capacity issue," thus the person just isn't able. Before you write someone off too quickly, make sure you've paid attention to the other performance needs they have.

- Have they received adequate training?
- Are your expectations clear?
- Is there a defined level of success?
- Does the person have the resources they need?
- Are there rewards for performance?
- Are you providing feedback and coaching?

There are certainly times when an employee is not the "right fit" for a position. But before we make that determination, we need to make sure we are doing our job first.

Take Action

Today during lunch, copy & paste the "seven areas" to a spreadsheet. Put the name of each of your employees across the columns. Take 6 minutes to assess the employees across the seven areas, using scales that make sense for you/your organization. Take another 7 minutes to analyze the data and make appropriate action plans.

Foggy Expectations

Do your employees ever "miss the mark?" Sometimes, do things get done in a manner you didn't expect or didn't want? Those are the times to hold back and first ask yourself, "where wasn't I clear?" Our first instinct is to often "blame the employee" and analyze what he or she did wrong. But as an effective manager, you also need to consider what you did wrong. Frequently, we haven't been clear in our expectations.

In addition to telling a person what to do, consider including what behaviors she needs to demonstrate to be successful. What else will she need to pay attention to, what a good job will "look like." With clear and specific expectations, including measurements and feedback, it is much more likely success will be achieved the first time.

Of course, make sure to document your clarifying expectations conversation so that you can offer praise to the employee during your next situational coaching opportunity. Or, if necessary, you are well prepared to take "appropriate corrective action."

Which Leader has the Most Potential?

The best approach in building a talent or leadership pipeline is to assess the *potential* of leaders against the level of sustained performance of them. It is critical that both perspectives of the leader are ascertained. The sustainability of performance at exceptional levels creates the pathway for a leader with potential to excel broadly and deeply for the good of the company. Exceptional performance alone, however, does not indicate future success.

A successful assessment of the potential of leaders against performance can prepare you and your company to determine a succession plan for key roles. Articulating, analyzing, and understanding potential also allows the company to properly invest in those leaders who offer the greatest opportunity to achieve a high return on investment of company resources focused on building leaders.

For those you identify as worthy of investment, consider these options.

- Advanced degree programs – executive MBAs, etc.
- Significant special projects/assignments
- Leadership development curriculum – internal and/or external
- Job/role rotation
- Mentoring
- Executive coaching

Succession Planning: Not Just For the Top Guys.

All seasoned leaders at one point in their careers have been challenged with the departure of a key employee who had certain work knowledge that was painful to replicate. Companies invest time and money in developing succession planning for leadership roles. They invest in developing strong leaders to make sure those employees are prepared to lead major functions of the business. But seldom is time invested to mitigate the risk of exposure from the loss of a key individual contributor.

Look at your teams' processes and key knowledge workers. Who has intimate knowledge of processes or data or customers that would not be easy to replace? Maybe the knowledge was built through years on the job. Maybe it's the combination of the individual's talents and skills. Maybe the function has been restructured to a point where a few folks do a tremendous amount of work.

Take an inventory of your mission-critical processes or information. Determine the truly critical from the really important. Next, visualize that the individual responsible for the process has just called you and said that for personal health reasons, they will not able to return to work. No transition. No knowledge transfer. No brain dump will be available. How painful – in business terms – will this be for your team and the organization?

Create an impact analysis. What is the dollar impact for:

- The loss of work from the process
- The loss of information
- The cost to hire 2 people to replace the one knowledgeable person
- Missed deadlines

- Overtime and/or overload

Take this information and figure out how to mitigate the risk before the tragedy. Document processes. Force cross training. Get an additional resource hired. Get other departments involved.

Or, figure out the story you'll spin for your boss for not mitigating the risks.

Play a Game

Looking for a creative and cheap way to practice your leadership skills? Be a kid again and play some games. Here are some game ideas and the associated skill areas.

- Blokus, Chess or Backgammon – strategic thinking, patience
- Charades – situational agility, team work
- Halo – executive politics
- Rock Band – team work
- Twister – relationship building
- Monopoly – winning it all . . . and putting it all back in the box
- Nerf Gun Wars – focusing, agility
- Scrabble – performance review terminology
- Settlers of Catan – budgeting, resource planning
- Wii Fit – stamina
- Risk – strategic thinking, execution, agility and decisiveness
- Bananagrams – creativity, flexibility, adjusting course

Gather a few peers, play a game and increase your leadership skills. And maybe you'll laugh a bit along the way.

Leverage Your Resident Experts

Your employees have resident expertise and knowledge that is likely to be valuable to others in the organization. Take some time to inventory the expertise and create a communication to market the expertise to others in the organization. Provide a "who to call list" to your internal customers which will highlight the strengths of your employees, allowing them some much desired notoriety and helping you to broadly sell your team's strengths to your peers and the organization as a whole.

This process might also yield insight for you as a leader.

- Are there gaps in backup coverage for key skill areas?
- Are any of your employees truly overloaded?
- Are there opportunities for cross training?

Take advantage of this project by having one of your employees take ownership to develop the list. Guide them on the process to ensure that the final product meets your quality standards and make sure to give them the credit.

#

Learning Moments

About The Author

Learning Moments

Michael Holland

Michael Holland unravels the mysteries of leadership. Michael is a professional executive coach and trusted advisor to executives who seek to become better leaders and build cohesive teams. Michael's wisdom and insight are the product of 25 plus years of leadership experience and an uncanny, natural ability to perceive the questions that need to be asked.

Michael founded Bishop House Consulting, Inc. in 1999 to provide organizational leadership expertise and team development services to companies experiencing dynamic change. Michael has provided distinguished executive coaching services to well over 300 leaders in organizations, ranging from start-ups to multi-billion dollar corporations. Michael earned his MBA from the University of Baltimore and is the author of *Leadership Learning Moments*, a weekly inspiration – or reminder – regarding the critical role leaders play in the lives of employees.

In addition to his role leading Bishop House Consulting, Michael serves on the Area Committee for Young Life Capital Region, invests his time and energy instigating men who seek more purpose in life, is a member of Grace Chapel of Clifton Park, and is active in the Burnt Hills, NY community where he lives with his wife and their three kids.

LinkedIn: www.linkedin.com/in/mikeatbishophouse

Persona blog: www.michaelsholland.com

Email: mike@bishophouse.com

Twitter: www.twitter.com/mikehollandatbh

Learning Moments

Bishop House Consulting, Inc.

Bishop House Consulting is the premier leadership development and organizational consulting firm working with companies in New York's Capital Region and Tech Valley. Founded by Michael Holland in 1999, the firm has grown steadily, maintaining trusted, long term relationships with clients. Bishop House coaches, trainers and consultants are well regarded as thought leaders in developing effective executives and managers, building cohesive teams, and navigating organizational change.

Bishop House Consulting helps leaders, teams and companies increase their effectiveness through exploration of personal communication styles and team dynamics with *Everything DiSC*® assessments and training solutions. Bishop House Consulting is an independent Authorized Distributor of *DiSC*® products and services.

www.BishopHouse.com

DiSC® *is a registered trademark of Inscape Publishing, Inc.*

Made in the USA
Charleston, SC
11 January 2013